MW00436162

A Decade of
Beach Walks

by
George Thatcher

QUAIL RIDGE PRESS
Brandon, Mississippi

Copyright ©2008 by George Thatcher

All Rights Reserved

No part of this book may be reproduced or utilized in any form or by any means, electronic or mechanical, including photocopying and recording, or by any information storage and retrieval system, without permission in writing from the publisher.

Library of Congress Cataloging-in-Publication Data

Thatcher, George 1922–
    A decade of beach walks / by George Thatcher.
        p. cm.
    ISBN-13: 978-1-934193-16-7
    ISBN-10: 1-934193-16-X
1. Nature. 2. Beaches. 3. Seasons. I. Title.
QH81.T3393 2008
508.314'6–dc22   2008008132

Front cover photo by Amanda McCoy, courtesy of the *Sun Herald*
Back cover photo by Dr. Donald Bradburn
Design by Cynthia Clark

Printed in Canada

QUAIL RIDGE PRESS

P. O. Box 123 • Brandon, Mississippi 39043
601-825-2063 • 800-343-1583 • www.quailridge.com

Dedication

To the wonderful cast of characters encountered on
a beach walk—the shorebirds, especially great blue herons
that bid us "Good day!" each morning.

To white morning glories with their golden throats and
to little fiddler crabs peeping from their burrows.

To mullets leaping from the sea and to noble ospreys flying
high overhead. And not to be forgotten are the busy
sanderlings at water's edge and hermit crabs nearby.

All are in God's marvelous domain.

Foreword

*W*hen Hurricane Katrina's record storm surge had receded on the afternoon of August 29, 2005, the physical world of south Mississippi was forever altered. Tens of thousands of the homes and businesses along this tranquil shore had been destroyed, and much of the cultural and architectural history of the region had been washed away. Indeed a great deal of the evidence of the storm could be seen on the seventy miles of beach that is the essence of this place. Virtually every foot of the beach was covered by the destruction wrought by the greatest natural disaster in American history.

The beach is also the world whose beauty has been captured in the enduring words of George Thatcher's daily column in the *Sun Herald*— words that have brought much hope and satisfaction to the paper's readers for more than ten years. Viewing the beach in those horrible days after Katrina, it was difficult not to despair. Certainly it was hard to imagine how the beach could ever be restored to its former vitality and beauty. But we learned that indeed it was possible through the methodical telling of its recovery. The chronicles of our beach-poet captured the cleansing that nature and time, with man in a minor partnership role, have achieved. We learned of the return of beach creatures, and through the prism of the poet, discovered the miracle that such teamwork can achieve.

By bearing witness to such a thing, George has helped inform us of more than the physical reformation on our shores, he has planted hope for tomorrow in our hearts, and has given evidence of what a communion of such a place through the gift of his words can do to lift our spirits.

—Stan Tiner
Vice President and Executive Editor of the
Sun Herald, a McClatchy newspaper
covering south Mississippi

Acknowledgments

This book represents the work of many wonderful people.

I am grateful to the *Sun Herald*, the McClatchy newspaper serving south Mississippi, for publishing my daily column, "Scenes from the Beach," since 1997. The newspaper was awarded the 2006 Pulitzer Gold Medal for Public Service for its heroic action in the aftermath of Hurricane Katrina that devastated our coastland in 2005. I particularly appreciate the wise and skilled editing of Marie Harris, the newspaper's opinion page editor, who transformed nearly 3,500 of my columns from sows' ears into silk purses. To Ricky Mathews, publisher; Stan Tiner, executive editor; and to the newspaper's dedicated staff, I extend heart-felt thanks for all that they have done through the years.

My gratitude, too, goes to Quail Ridge Press, a remarkable publishing company, that has grown from inception thirty years ago at the kitchen table of Gwen and Barney McKee into a thriving national enterprise. Theirs is a great American success story! Quail Ridge Press, "a pearl of great value," deserves to be treasured for its important contributions. To Gwen and Barney, to Cyndi Clark (the wonderfully talented art director who planned and created, not only this book, but also my three previous ones), and to Quail Ridge's fine staff, I express high esteem and sincerest gratitude.

We are indebted to Dr. Donald Bradburn of New Orleans for the back cover photograph. He is a renowned nature photographer, conservationist, and a cherished friend.

George Thatcher
Spring 2008

Introduction

*T*hroughout my long life, walking the beach has been far more than a diversion for me. It is an integral part of who I am, an activity that marks my persona, surpassing favorite pastimes of tennis, chess and reading, all of which I enjoy daily.

The shore is an elemental setting for walking. The immensity of the sea with its diurnal tides, breaking waves that bring brine to one's lips, the feel of the wind against one's face, clouds racing overhead, sunrises and sunsets, a canopy of stars and planets at night, shorebirds and other beach creatures—all have been a lifelong attraction for me down the corridor of years, and they still are.

The lure of the beach has been for me a mythic call of the Sirens, as reported by Homer. It is there along the shore that I feel united with the natural world, touched by reality. Surrounded by palpable things that enliven the senses, at times I find myself in the company of time-less people, like Henry David Thoreau, Ralph Waldo Emerson, Emily Dickinson, John Muir and others, all wonderful companions with whom to share a walk.

It is there on the beach in solitary walks that one has an intimation of how the world looked at the time of creation. So it is, that a walk frequently becomes a spiritual experience, imparting a certain aware-ness that it is the Creator who spreads the expanse of natural beauty before us.

This is the fourth and final book of selections from my daily columns in the *Sun Herald*, the McClatchy newspaper serving south

Mississippi. Now in its eleventh consecutive year of publication, the column has appeared six times a week, more than three thousand times.

Its longevity comes as a surprise both to the writer and to the newspaper. Who would have thought in 1997, when the first column was published, that it would have lasted for more than a decade? I am humbly grateful to the newspaper's readers and book buyers who have responded enthusiastically through the years. The column still continues each day and may be accessed Sundays through Fridays on the Internet at www.sunherald.com.

Each column recounts a beach walk taken that day, a report of things seen or experienced. Sometimes, too, it is a telling of thoughts that come to mind during the saunter.

The beach on which I walk is a beautiful strand of white sand on the Mississippi Sound, on the northern curve of the Gulf of Mexico. It is an area steeped in history. It was here that d'Iberville landed in 1699, establishing Biloxi as the capital of French America, two decades before the founding of New Orleans. Just offshore, on the barrier islands, the British assembled to attack New Orleans in the War of 1812. Here, too, during the Civil War, Union forces constructed a large, military fort that still stands. It is a place also where fishermen harvest an abundance of sea life. It is a cornucopia of huge, commercial quantities of shrimp, crabs, oysters and fish.

Our beach is urban, not far removed from the bustle of the modern world. People sometimes ask if I would not prefer a more secluded, deserted one on the barrier islands. Of course, the answer is yes. But there are advantages to our beach. Its accessibility is unmatched. Within moments of leaving my front door, I am on the beach, ready for the day's walk. During autumn, winter and spring there are few people here. Even in summer, early mornings and late afternoons often find the beach deserted. The sounds of civilization—a passing train, highway traffic, an overhead airplane, a speedboat—while sometimes heard, may be dismissed from the mind, allowing a walker complete solitude.

Our beach, a frontier where land and sea meet, is a remarkably pleasant place in every season.

Now in my 86th year, I have walked along this same shore for many decades. Occasionally, the question is asked, "Don't you tire of the same scenery every day?" "No," I reply. Each day's walk is a new and different adventure. As Heraclitus said, "You cannot step into the same river twice." Change occurs daily. I always wake in anticipation of another interesting day. Never tiring of repetition, I expect discoveries, little epiphanies—a hidden wildflower, a different seashell, driftwood, jellyfish, a snowy egret, a nicely shaped cloud. Each day holds its own particular treasure.

A usual day begins with my awaking at five o'clock to morning prayer, a Spartan breakfast, early Mass, tennis, a beach walk, coffee with friends at the local drug store, lunch, an afternoon of reading and writing and evenings filled with social events—a busy and good life. The Lord has given me good health. Fortunately, I take no medicines, despite my advanced years.

Any time of day is good for a beach walk. My preferences are sunrise and sunset, but there is much to be said for other times, too. The shoreline is active at high tide, when detritus arrives at water's edge for hungry shorebirds, but there are also special discoveries at low tide when acres of sand flats, usually submerged, are exposed. It is then that one can walk dry-shod on the ribbed bottoms, observing countless communities of burrowing sea worms and shellfish.

Allow me to add a word about the speed of walking. There are people who walk for physical exercise, reaching high numbers of paces per minute. Although exercise is a byproduct of my walks, it is not the prime motivation.

My pace is more of a saunter, which gives more opportunity to see and hear. Rarely do I exceed 86 steps a minute (that long-honored rate for infantrymen on long marches), lessened by interruptions to see a wildflower or to observe a butterfly.

Today's Walk

It is a few minutes before sunrise on a mild autumn day. I sit on the seawall, awaiting full daylight. Consider, if you will, how different this shore may have been on a day like this three centuries ago before the French colonizers had arrived. My guess is that it was pretty much the same as it is this morning. Nature has a way of renewing and restoring things. The beach today, the one in 1699, and even shores like this one on the day of creation—all bear a similarity, I think. It is the same sun and moon, the same sea. The horizon this morning is empty of ships. Admittedly, there are many human footprints on the sand, but little else has changed.

The beach's primal, elemental character is an appeal that continually beckons me and other walkers to this sandy strand.

Now that the sun has risen, come along with me on today's beach walk. We begin by reciting the psalmist's words, "This is the day the Lord hath made; we will rejoice and be glad in it."

Standing in shallow water in the flats is a great blue heron. We always bid the stately bird, "Good day," and he often nods his head in polite reply.

Flying eastward toward the rising sun is a line of nine brown pelicans, one after another, in formation. Soon we will see them return, winging their way to the west. We name the pelicans "the dawn patrol," remembering the old World War I aviation movie.

Roosting on the beach are flocks of gulls at rest along with several black skimmers, terns and a few pigeons. They patiently await high tide to begin foraging for food at water's edge.

An ebbed tide today has stranded a number of comb jelly-fish on the exposed, wet sand. See them glistening like diamonds in the bright sunshine. We hope that the incoming tide will float the jellies to safety in deep water.

Inspect, for a moment, the little, round holes in the sand. These are entrances to burrows, dug by fiddler crabs seeking protection from hungry shorebirds. Soon they will hibernate for the winter, slumbering until spring.

At water's edge is an overturned horseshoe crab, seemingly dead after laying hundreds of eggs in the wet sand last night. We flip the crab over, and thankfully watch as it crawls away safely, disappearing into the sea.

Precisely on schedule, a highlight of the morning's walk appears. A snowy egret, the most beautiful of all our shorebirds, gambols happily in the shallows, pursuing minnows.

Now we walk along the wrack line, yesterday's high tide mark, where the sea deposits its treasures—driftwood, shells

and other things, like fishing lures, cigarette filters and trash.
Let's scavenge for a while, as we walk along the wrack line
back to the seawall.

The shoreline—the sand and the sea—is filled with living
things today, but it has not always been so.

When I reached the beach two days after Hurricane Katrina
in 2005, it was devastated. A dreadful silence had settled on
the shore. Bodies of dead shorebirds were everywhere, lying in
mute testimony of the disaster that had befallen us. Not a liv-
ing creature was seen. Particularly, I recall the lifeless body of a
great blue heron draped grotesquely across the top step of the
seawall. The beach itself was littered with stools, tables, chairs,
washing machines, refrigerators and the like. All along the
shore, there were scenes of annihilation, as if from Dante's
Inferno. *It was a time of sorrow, a time of weeping.*

However, only days later shorebirds returned, a few gulls
at first, then black skimmers and a pelican or two appeared.
After a month, nearly all species had been restored, but in
reduced numbers. Although the beach was still littered with
debris, recovery of the natural world had begun. I remember
the unexpected joy of finding a lone, yellow wildflower, a gold-
en aster, in full bloom by the seawall. The flower sent forth a
message of rebirth. The beach was indeed healing.

Then appeared the welcomed, incoming flights of birds on
their autumnal migration, landing on the beach, as they had in
past seasons. One wonders if they were shocked at the condi-
tion of our ravaged beach, so different from the one they had
left in the spring on their northward flight.

Nature was now in full control of the recovery, redeeming the beach quickly from the mortal blow that it had suffered.

"You may drive out nature with a pitchfork," rightly observed Horace, the Roman poet, 2,000 years ago, "but it will always come charging back."

And, so it did! Hurricane Katrina brutally punished our coastal beaches, but soon nature was at work with its blessed restoration and renewal.

We know that the beach has almost fully recovered, and we celebrate its rebirth. However, there are a few worrisome things still missing.

For example, before the hurricane, long strands of whelk egg cases were frequently found at water's edge. The empty cases gave assurance that new generations of whelks had been spawned. Now, however, no cases lie along the shoreline, raising questions about the survival of the whelk population.

A bird missing since the hurricane, a favorite of mine, is the blue belted kingfisher. With hope, I look for its return each day.

Of course, these are but minor losses when compared with the beach's heroic redemption. I propose a toast to Mother Nature!

A suggestion to readers . . .

In perusing the following selections, allow me to suggest that you read only one or two at a sitting, keeping in mind that each represents a single day's walk. Reading multiple walks at one time distorts, not only the original experience, but also adversely affects the meaning that the passages impart. Unlike other books, this journal should be read sparingly.

The Beach in
Autumn

There is a particular pleasure, but difficult to explain, in walking along a shoreline unmarked by other footprints. Such a walk may occur early in the morning after tide and wind have erased all previous footprints and swept trash away. It is then that this portion of the world seems to be in a primeval state, unsullied, undefiled. Lasting only briefly after sunrise, the walk ends with the beginning of the day's activity on the beach.

*A*t first light, before sunrise, a sail appears
on the distant horizon, reaching for port. The
boat is "hull down," so far away that only the
sail is visible. In earlier times, how many emo-
tions have ignited at the sight of a sail! Wives,
mothers, sisters, lovers—how many countless
women scanned horizons for the return of
their men! The boat, now in full view,
"hull-up," is a sloop at the end of
an enjoyable night's sail.

*T*oday's radiant sunrise follows yesterday's majestic sunset. What words can describe the scenes? About 3,000 years ago, a psalmist put it this way, "The heavens declare the glory of God; the skies proclaim the work of his hands. . . ." It is a silent message, the psalmist writes; there are no words or sounds.* Yet a message is conveyed from one day to another that there is Godly order and balance and beauty in the world for all to see.

*Psalm 19.

T.S. Eliot wrote that some blooms had "the look of flowers that are looked at."* The pale, yellow blossom found on the sand dune this morning does not have that look. I think that I am the only person to see the wildflower and perhaps the only one who will ever see it. It grows hidden among tall stands of grass. Yet, as Wordsworth phrased it, the most insignificant flower "can give thoughts that do often lie too deep for tears."**

*"Burnt Norton" by T.S. Eliot.
**"Intimations of Immortality" by William Wordsworth.

*D*une grasses are preparing for winter.
Although thermometers still record summer
temperatures, plants in the depths of their
beings somehow know the change of seasons.
Sap, rising in the spring to reach the topmost
leaf and the highest seed, now begins to
recede a bit. You can see it retreat in a

slight browning of the
higher leaves and in
brittleness of seeds.
Soon sap will descend
deep into the roots,
retiring into its
winter quarters.

*T*hink of Homer today, as we walk along the shore. The  first known European writer had a profound appreciation of the sea, although he was blind. His phrases still haunt our minds, "west wind that sang along the wine-dark sea, . . . plough the watery deep, . . . driving sand, . . . rosy-fingered dawn, . . . the shore of the sounding sea, . . . ocean the source of all," and more. Now, nearly 3,000 years later, we remember the artistry of his words.*

Iliad by Homer, written about 850 B.C.

On this warm autumn afternoon, it is pleasant to watch a pair of common loons swimming offshore on the surface of a glass-like, calm sea. There they swim together, a stately pair, heads held regally aloft, their long bills horizontal. From time to time one dives, the other remaining on the surface. Nearby are other diving birds, double-crested cormorants. Floating on the surface too, the cormorants hold their bills at a higher angle than do loons.

There is a shrimp boat close to shore, plying the early morning sea, spreaders outstretched. Probably it seeks white shrimp, ones that are sometimes in the Sound late in the season. Through binoculars the crew can be seen on deck, working the nets. If asked, they would reply that they are shrimping for the money it brings, but I think, too, it is a siren song, the appeal of the sea, and the joy of being afloat that keeps them there.

It is a short walk from my home to the beach, but the hour before dawn (it is said to be the darkest of the night) makes it seem farther. The silence is broken by doleful cooing of mourning doves, awaking even before the cardinals. A neighbor's dog barks only once. Perhaps he recognizes me. Light from the new moon is diffused by a cloud bank. At the shore, black skimmers are heard barking in the shallows as they fish in the darkness.

*T*oday begins with sunrise, an orange ball partially obscured by the eastern horizon, yet casting color on distant clouds above the western
horizon. Mentally, we intone Dostoyevsky's
classic plea, "Love all God's creation, the
whole and every grain of sand of it. Love
every leaf, every ray of God's light. Love the
animals; love the plants;
love everything. If you love
everything, you will per-
ceive the divine mystery
in things. . . ."*

*The Brothers Karamazov by Fyodor Dostoyevsky.

*T*here is a passage in Anne Morrow Lindbergh's Gift from the Sea *that I read from time to time, "One becomes . . . bare, open, empty as the beach, erased by today's tides of all yesterday's scribblings. . . ." The shore will produce its treasures in its own time. "The sea does not reward those who are too anxious. . . . Patience, patience, patience is what the sea teaches. Patience and faith . . . ," she discovered.**

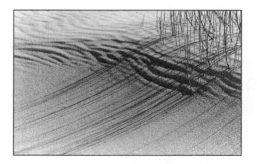

**Gift from the Sea* by Anne Morrow Lindbergh; Pantheon Books, New York (1983).

*A*mong the first shorebirds to fly away when humans approach are black skimmers. Far more wary than gulls or some terns, they have retained their independence and wildness. Never ones to scavenge, skimmers fish for their food. Their self-sufficiency ensures that they will not become domesticated like pigeons, city dwellers now, living on the dole, but once proud, wild, self-reliant creatures soaring the lofty cliffs.

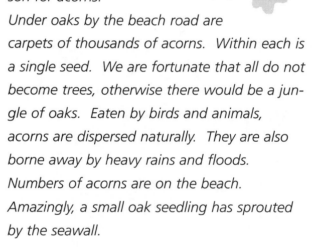

This autumn has been a bountiful season for acorns. Under oaks by the beach road are carpets of thousands of acorns. Within each is a single seed. We are fortunate that all do not become trees, otherwise there would be a jungle of oaks. Eaten by birds and animals, acorns are dispersed naturally. They are also borne away by heavy rains and floods. Numbers of acorns are on the beach. Amazingly, a small oak seedling has sprouted by the seawall.

*W*ispy, cirrus clouds, high above the sea, are moving westward at a fast pace, far fleeter than the mild east wind at beach level. Luke Howard, the scientist who named clouds in the 19th century, thought that clouds like the ones overhead looked like locks of a child's hair. So he aptly named them cirrus, the Latin word for "curl." Indeed like strands of hair, our clouds are a joy to watch on this pleasant autumn day.

*W*hen high tide occurs at night, horseshoe crabs come ashore in darkness to lay eggs at water's edge. The survival rate of such eggs rises far above those laid in daytime. During daylight hours, while crabs are in the act of burrowing into the wet sand, laying eggs, shorebirds stand nearby eagerly awaiting a feast. However, when eggs are laid in the dark, a time when no birds are present, their life expectancy increases.

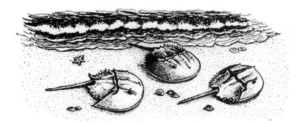

Shorebirds are not known for singing, although in courtship, gulls do utter pleasing sounds. Mostly, however, shorebirds' voices are used for the purpose of alarm—strident, shrill calls aimed at warning the flock of imminent danger. As people near a roost, skimmers are first to bark the alarm, "kak, kak, kak." Then gulls vent an excited, "ha, ha, ha, ha," followed by terns whistling, "toureee," and the plaintive voices of plovers, "peooeee."

*F*ar down the beach stroll two young lovers, pausing now and again to embrace, stopping too to record their love in sand messages.

They bring to mind words from a poem by Gary Snyder: ". . . Waves and the prevalent  easterly breeze, whispering into you, through us, the grace."* It is about the grace of human love that he writes, truly a gift. The couple walks toward the seawall, and I choose to leave their other sand scribblings unread.

*Quoted in *Repossessing and Renewing* by Sherman Paul, Louisiana State University Press (1976).

Never adept at definitive bird identification, I have been pondering the identity of a shorebird for several days.

Is it an immature great blue heron, or is it a little blue heron? An experienced birder would know immediately, but I suspend judgment until authoritative guidebooks are consulted back home this afternoon. The heron wades gracefully in shallow water, fully confident of who he is, even if I am not.

This is the season when mullets gather together in huge schools, much to the delight of throw-net fishermen who catch a dozen or so in a single cast. There are two schools in the shallows now, easy to spot because the fish are near the surface. The mullets in one school are in a dense formation, their snouts protruding out of the water. Measuring a foot or so in size, the mullets, underappreciated delicacies, would grace any table.

"*It is more important to feel than it is to know,*" *wrote Rachel Carson in her book* A Sense of Wonder,* *instructing children to appreciate nature. While it is helpful to know why a mullet comes near shore at this season, perceiving the fish itself and feeling its leap to escape a predator is the essence of appreciation. To know that clouds are blown by the wind is good, but quite another thing to allow your mind to soar with them.*

*Quoted in *Fishcamp* by Nancy Lord; Island Press/Shearwater Books, Washington, D.C. (1997).

*S*ulphur butterflies abound
on the sand dune this morning.
Their sunny color may be the reason why the
insects were named butterflies. One very
active sulphur (a male, I guess, because it is
larger) lights for a moment on a scrap of
yellow paper, thinking it to be another sulphur.
There was a similar incident yesterday when an
alfalfa butterfly pursued a bouncing tennis
ball, attracted by its yellow color, mistaking it
for a female sulphur.

The day began in silence, a majestic symphony, like Mozart's Requiem, *which the audience does not hear at first but after a bit listens to a growing, dramatic crescendo. At sunrise, the sea was flatly calm, making no sound, not even lapping noises. In the distance could be seen ripples, a sign that wind was disturbing the surface. By mid-morning, whitecaps were coming ashore, breaking with a rumbling sound, rolling high onto the beach.*

Winds cleanse the beach. Today's gale has not only erased the footprints of both bird and man, it has blown away debris—candy wrappers and other trash, as well as fallen leaves from trees near the beach road. Some heavier things, like the skeletal remains of a catfish on the wrack line, are buried under layers of sand. Creating lines on the beach, the wind traces elongated patterns of energy, identical to those under water on the wave-ribbed bottom of the sea.

*A*fter yesterday's roiling waves, fierce winds and turbulence, the sea this morning is pacific—that is pacific with a small "p," not the capital "P" that Magellan used when  he first named the Pacific Ocean. After encountering typhoons later in the voyage, one wonders if he regretted calling it "peaceful." Our sea today is markedly changed. Gentle waves lap the shore. But dare we forget the "tiger heart that pants beneath it"?*

Moby Dick by Herman Melville.

*T*oday large flocks of black skimmers gather near the fishing pier, nearly 400 of the shorebirds placidly at roost. When a walker approaches, one skimmer sounds alarm, sending entire flocks aloft, wheeling as if they were one bird. Each skimmer implicitly, without hesitation, follows the leadership of one bird. In some manner, there is instant communication of the command to flee sent to the flocks. Not one bird dissents.

*W*hen the wind is high, as it is today, lines on beached sailboats slap against the masts, creating euphonious sounds, pleasant to the ears of every sailor. It is a perpetual angelus, agreeable music. In earlier years, masts and spars were made of wood. Then the sounds were somewhat different than those from modern aluminum masts, but the tempo was the same. The measured notes are now the same cadence once heard by Homer and Columbus.

There is a remarkable indication of new life in trees after the hurricane. Although it is autumn and a season when tree leaves should be browning and falling to the ground, some trees—pecan and live oaks—are putting out new growth. I watch in wonder as tender, green leaves appear on otherwise leafless branches. It is nature's message to us that life does go on, despite the wounds sustained from tempest winds and flooding seawater. It is a signal to us like the fabled Phoenix of old, rising from ashes, and like the rainbow that Noah witnessed after the Great Flood.

*A*long the pathway to the beach this morning, I encountered a cluster of arresting blue flowers in a garden by a home that is no longer standing, a victim of the recent hurricane. A common name for the species is Mexican petunia. Sometimes it is called ruellia. Regardless of its name, the blue blossoms brighten my day, a reminder of the garden's former beauty.

The melodic trill of
a mockingbird, singing
prettily at dawn in the trees
bordering the battered beach
road, is a welcomed sound.
America's only nightingales, mockingbirds are
known not only for their tuneful songs, but
also for their mimicking of other birds and animals. After greeting today's sunrise, the bird
uttered a mimicry of squirrel sounds. At first I
thought that it was in fact a squirrel in the oak
tree, so true was the bird's parody. The hurricane has taken a severe toll on the squirrel
population. Since the tempest, not one has
been seen near the beach road.

One positive thing that the hurricane taught us is a need to simplify our lives. The loss of homes and possessions teaches us that we had acquired far too much stuff, things that we did not need and didn't use. For me, today's beach walk is instructive. I find that I don't need binoculars and bird guides to enjoy watching shorebirds or to fully enjoy a pleasant autumn day. In fact, I don't even need shoes. The sand feels good beneath bare feet!

There are important lessons to be learned from the behavior of trees. Along the beach road most limbs are now leafless—leaves, nuts and flowers blown off by tempestuous winds. Immediately after the hurricane the trees looked as if it were mid-winter. Now green sprouts appear—a second springtime! Think of the trees, too, during the hurricane— how they bent with each gust, complying mostly but not breaking.

Two lessons for us:
Be resilient, bend
with the wind, and
then after the storm
begin a new life.

In one of his treatises,* Thoreau complained that half of his walk was spent retracing the steps that he had taken earlier, because one must return to his point of origin. We have found a partial solution to the problem. Take today's walk as an example. From the point of origin, the walk is at water's edge, viewing the shoreline and the sea. Upon returning, one walks along the wrack line, observing the countless treasures to be found there.

*Walking by Henry David Thoreau; The Portable Thoreau, Penguin Books, New York (1977).

On the wrack line, that assemblage of debris brought ashore by the most recent high tide, is the branch of an elderberry tree. The discovery brings to mind the making of chinaberry popguns when I was a boy. A hollow elderberry branch was the gun's barrel; the plunger, a carved broomstick, propelled chinaberries long distances. Holding the elderberry branch in hand, for a moment I relive happy, childhood memories of chinaberry wars.

The autumnal equinox marks a time when the hours of daylight and darkness are evenly balanced. From now until the winter solstice at year's end, the hours of darkness will increase. Sunset will come a bit earlier each day and the sun will rise a bit later each morning. The changing season and increasing darkness affect our moods. We love the day's brightness and don't relish "the dying of the light,"* as Dylan Thomas eloquently put it.

*"Do not go gentle into that good night" by Dylan Thomas (1914–1953).

A very old brown pelican occupies a nearby
offshore post every day. Hoary with age,
the bird has white plumage on its head and
long neck. It is "ancient of days," to use a
biblical expression. Unlike other pelicans
that peer downward to spot fish swimming
below before plunging after them, he sits on
his haunches, contemplating the world.
We have named the ancient
pelican Socrates.

*A*utumn sunsets above our western horizon are spectacular scenes, especially as night approaches. "Exquisitely dying," is how Aldous Huxley described their beauty.* Today's sunset emblazons the entire sky in rich crimson colors. There is too much grandeur for words. Along with Job, I feel that "I have spoken of great things which I have not understood, things too wonderful for me to know."**

*"Ninth Philosopher's Song" by Aldous Huxley.
**Job 42:3.

Autumn Leaves (haiku)

Autumn leaves tumble
here and there in the north wind,
forgetting summer.

A field north of the beach is filled with butterflies this morning. October is a good month for viewing them when days are warm, dry, and sunny. Nabokov once observed butterflies "collapsing in laughter" on a sunflower.* The butterflies are happy here today too, flitting among the wildflowers. He compared the colorful insects with seraphs, angelic beings from celestial realms associated with light and purity. And so they are!

*Nabokov's Butterflies by Vladimir Nabokov; Beacon Press, Boston (2000).

*V*isitors to our beach this morning are two great egrets, elegantly white shorebirds with striking yellow bills and black legs and feet. This is our first sighting of the egrets since the hurricane struck two years ago. Their slender bodies move with grace as they walk in the shallows. They are greeted hospitably, not only by walkers, but also by our resident heron that joins them in their stroll. The egrets have animated the stoic, silent heron.

Autumn is a season of transition. Summer, when life was at its fullest, has gradually ended. The change is perceptible. By degrees, sea life, so obvious and plentiful near the shore in the warm months, has retreated into deeper water. Mullets, having leaped so frequently in the shallows, have withdrawn. Some shorebirds have migrated southward. Profuse only weeks ago, many wildflowers have now closed their petals. Nature prepares for winter.

*F*illed with hundreds of butterflies again today, the field is alive
with the colorful, fluttering creatures. What a
pageant of natural beauty! It is difficult to
remember that once these exquisite butterflies
were ugly caterpillars. They live too briefly,
spanning a cycle from egg to caterpillar to
chrysalis, reaching adulthood, then dying soon.
Yet today full of life, that spark of Godhood,
butterflies bring us lasting joy.

A herring gull with a dislocated right wing has captured our attention for several days now. Grounded, unable to fly, the gull handles its physical disability with grace. The bird is not impeded from walking and demonstrates agility in moving rapidly across the sand. Foraging at water's edge, the gull takes care of itself nicely, despite a dangling wing. Today it walks on a nearby parking lot, finding scraps of discarded food there.

*R*oosting shorebirds are skittishly nervous creatures. When beach walkers approach, their first inclination is to react to the walkers as predators and fly away. After years of trial, I have learned how to pass roosting birds without evicting them. The secret is to walk slowly, deliberately making no sudden move. Hands are better left in pockets; eyes look straight ahead. Sometimes a skimmer may fly away, however most birds remain watchful, but at rest.

A one-sided conversation with a fiddler crab:
"See here, fiddler, don't you know that you
have dug your burrow in a very perilous loca-
tion? Look at all the hungry gulls, waiting for
you to show yourself. And that is not the only
danger. Listen to the loud, beach tractors,
plowing up the sand nearby. Who would sell
you a life insurance policy at this site? Now, if
you dig your burrow on a sand dune, you will
be safer. Are you listening, fiddler?"

*B*utterflies are flying west today in large numbers, mostly monarchs, and fritillaries, including some sulphurs, all following the shoreline. Nearing their time to migrate, the butterflies will soon rise to heights sufficient to find prevailing north winds to carry them southward to Mexico. Their casualties in passage across the Gulf will be staggering. But for now, there is no thought of failure, as they briskly fly nearer their distant, winter home.

$\mathcal{A}$ lone, comb jellyfish is stranded this morning on an exposed sandbar in the shallows. Surely, it is one of the Lord's humblest 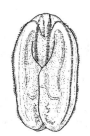 creatures, an animal in a lower phylum of creation. For a while, we watch its gelatinous, striped body lying there, transparent, revealing the sandbar beneath it. With no brain, of course, the jelly cannot think, but it senses light through a system of nerves. Touching it, one feels its soft, fragile body, pulsating with life.

*A*gainst my better judgment, for a few days I have been feeding bread to a wounded gull, the one suffering from a broken right wing. Unable to fly, the bird had been fending for itself, foraging for food at water's edge and elsewhere near the beach. Previously, my practice has been not to intervene in situations like this. Nature handles things very well without outside help. Now the injured gull awaits my arrival at the beach every morning.

$\mathcal{T}$hings look civilized on the beach this afternoon. Gulls bask in the sun; skimmers fish offshore; fiddler crabs scurry about—all enjoy a pleasant autumn day. We often forget that the creatures we encounter are wild animals. The sand shark, chasing fish in the shallows, is as ferocious as a lion in an African jungle. Docile shorebirds survive by their brutal instincts. We do not criticize their behavior,

but simply recognize its primitive origin.

*A*fter torrential rains, like those experienced this week, frogs are sometimes seen along the shore. Frogs, you say, on the beach? Yes, but they do not usually reside in our sandy biotope. Their presence is explained by rainwater rushing through drainage systems, carrying them unwillingly from their habitat on the mainland. Found at water's edge this morning is a frog, very much alive, but out of its element, surviving in an alien environment.

*A*fter the recent, heavy rains, the wrack line on the beach (that mark left by high tides and accumulated refuse) is filled with interesting objects today. Some driftwood has been sculpted into works of art by waves. Numerous empty clam and oyster shells have been dumped here by the sea. But most interesting is a short length of a ship's thick hawser, or mooring rope, out of which grows a pine seedling, six inches tall, its needles remarkably green and healthy.

"*Calling all butterflies of every race from source unknown . . . ,*" *intoned Robert Frost in a delightful verse.* It is indeed as if the butterflies had heard the summons today, because in numbers they are visiting beach wildflowers. A monarch or two, a few gulf fritillaries, and several sulphurs flutter among weedy plants by the seawall, selecting blooms here and there to visit. One large yellow butterfly alights briefly on a tall, wafting stem of sea oats.*

*"Pod of the Milkweed," *The Poetry of Robert Frost*; Henry Holt & Company, New York (1979).

*A*mong a myriad of butterflies fluttering along the shoreline this afternoon is a colorful, gulf fritillary, named for nodding flowers with spotted petals. Obviously tired, the little creature has settled down to rest upon a mound of sand, its tinted wings raised and joined in repose. There it remains, wafting in the mild sea breeze. Your scribe watches the butterfly from the bottom step of the seawall where he too sits in fatigue after a long beach walk.

*I*n late autumn I sojourn to North Carolina, the guest of close friends at their gracious home, "The Sheepfold," on Big Sheep Cliff Mountain. My time-honored goal each year is to climb the mountain, a daunting challenge. I struggled along, past the continental divide, up sheer inclines to the crest. I have noticed that each year the mountain gets steeper. My hosts have urged me not to report the change, a geologic phenomenon, to the authorities.

*I*t is a sure sign of late autumn when loons return. A flotilla of five floats today only a few yards off shore. Winter residents here, loons are large, black, aquatic birds, known for their diving skills. Indeed, in Europe their common name is "diver." They suddenly dive, remaining under water for long periods, surfacing far away. The likeness of our common loon is engraved on Canadian one-dollar coins that they call "loonies."

*I*t is the end of a lovely autumn day on the beach. A day, you say, like the succession of all previous days since creation? Each day is different, because this is the Great Now. Real things are happening. Gulls fly overhead; waves break against the shore. All the past corridors of days exist only in memory; all the future ones to infinity lie entirely within our minds. But today, gulls fly; waves break; we breathe and think in a moment of happy reality.

The Beach in
Winter

It is an icy morning on the beach. A piercing north wind, punishing face and hands, propels the sea southward far beyond the limits of the low tide that occurs at the moment. Underfoot, at water's edge, crystals of ice crunch at each step. In large flocks, gulls roost close to one another on the sand beach, but the larger shorebirds—herons, pelicans and cormorants—are nowhere to be seen. After the shortest of beach walks this year, I too leave.

I stand on what had been the threshold of a fine beach home before the hurricane. The old homestead is gone, as are its occupants—all gone but not forgotten. The family that had lived here was among the town's early settlers, prominent in their time. The wide veranda, overlooking the sea, once resounded with laughter and happy voices. Now there is only silence, except for wind passing through branches of the surviving oaks.

A lugworm has crawled out of its burrow in the wet sand. Normally, the lug lives an upside-down existence, its head at the bottom of the tunnel. But, now, completely exposed, lying flat on the sand, the worm is in full daylight, maybe for the first time in its life. What must the lug think of a world never before seen? Now it nimbly vanishes, once again descending into its sandy burrow, perhaps to dream of the wondrous things seen on its excursion.

At water's edge is a small piece of drift-wood, encrusted with four acorn barnacles.  Having absorbed seawater during its long journey, the wood is wet and heavy. The driftwood's parasites, the four barnacles, are still alive, because their host had been beached only a short time. If left high and dry for a few hours, the barnacles would surely die. We toss the driftwood back into the water, hoping that a current will carry it and its occupants away.

A simple, small magnifying glass transforms a winter beach into Lilliputian landscapes. A petal on a scraggly aster bloom by the seawall becomes an expanse of yellow velvet. Dragon-like, a black ant (late in the season for insects) crawls atop the flower's disk. Stalks of grass look like giant tree trunks. A handful of sand turns into crystalline boulders with jagged edges. The tiny, perfectly aligned teeth of a seashell are an orthodontist's dream.

A dense fog envelops the beach, reducing visibility to only a few steps. Separating walkers from the outside world, the fog isolates us, shorebirds and humans. We walk through the fog at water's edge, seeing only a footfall or two ahead. Out of the gloom comes a nearby birdcall. "Tooo-lee, tooo-a-lee," the unseen bird cries, the voice of a black-bellied plover that we unknowingly may have flushed from its feeding grounds on the sand flats.

*P*eople view things differently. It happens right here in our own community. Some value trees; others don't care much about them. A couple of hundred years ago, William Blake wrote, ". . . The tree which moves some to tears of joy is in the eyes of others only a green thing that stands in the way." There is a particular oak near the beach road, its starkly bare, wounded limbs uplifted. Does anyone else see its anguish?

A strong east wind, gusting to thirty knots, buffets the beach. Under gray, rain clouds, the sea is filled with whitecaps. Each off-shore post is occupied by a pelican, precarious-ly perched there. Leaning into the wind, the pelicans perform balancing acts, changing their stance with each variance of the wind. Usually they cant their heads downward to see fish swimming below, but not today. Merely keeping their balance is a task in itself.

*S*cientists have studied the fiddler crab and have given it a Latin name, *Uca minax,* and have positioned it in the Animalia kingdom. Its phylum is Arthropoda; its class, Malacostraca; its order, Decapoda; its family, Ocypodidae. Allow me to comment that you don't need all this exact information and technical knowledge to joyfully watch a little fiddler romp across the beach. In fact, the Latin names may actually impede your fun.

*A*n unpleasant day! Piercingly penetrating, the wind nips at face and ears. Waves come ashore from a slate-colored sea, sending a salty spray to one's lips. Now, from an overcast sky, a light rain falls. Having sought sanctuary elsewhere, not a shorebird is seen. It is precisely as Emily Dickinson once wrote, in a delightful verse. ". . . Nature, like us, is sometimes caught without her diadem."

Collected Poems of Emily Dickinson, Gramercy Books, New York (1982).

*I*n his book, Compass, *Alan Gurney reminds us how very limited vision is at sea.* For example, a sailor standing on the deck of a ship, his eyes nine feet above sea level, can see only about seven miles. Climbing a 75-foot mast, he can then see 20 miles. At water's edge, vision is even shorter, because our eyes are only five feet above sea level. We don't see the barrier island, nine miles away; we merely see the tops of the island's tall pines.*

*Compass by Alan Gurney; W.W. Norton & Company, New York (2004).

*T*he flat, mirror-like surface of the sea today was marred only by ripples caused by the bill of a black skimmer fishing near shore. The radiating ripples soon disappear, erasing all evidence that the bird had flown there. Again, the sea is flatly calm. On his deathbed, John Keats considered words for his tombstone. "Here lies," he wrote, "one whose name was writ in water."* He thought that he would soon be forgotten, as is today's skimmer.

*Inscription in the Keats-Shelley Museum in Rome, Italy.

A cool, north wind causes the tall panic grass by the seawall to bend and wave in a rhythm determined by each gust. Not as pliable as they were in summer, the brown stalks still move with some dexterity and beauty. Their motion would be a suitable accompaniment to the winter move-ment of Vivaldi's Four Seasons *or to Handel's* Water Music. *Like ballerinas, the stalks of tall grass become wands of grace in the wind.*

*T*he waves coming ashore this morning bring with them an assortment of small pebbles. Rolling up on the beach, the pebbles follow breaking waves, rolling far onto the sand, but never reaching as far as does the water itself. When the waves break and rush seaward, the receding water carries the pebbles back, too. So it becomes an incessant exercise in futility— little brown stones rolling up the beach onto wet sand, then retreating headlong.

*I*n the year of his death, 1862, Henry David Thoreau wrote an essay about walking.* A simple pleasure, he said, walking is an art that most people don't understand. He stressed the importance of "sauntering," walking at a leisurely pace, strolling. Walking merely for exercise or health, Thoreau wrote, is a mistake, because one should amble along musing only about nature. So it is that today I saunter along the shore, thinking about Thoreau.

*Walking by Henry David Thoreau; Penguin Books; New York (1995).

*B*each walking lends itself nicely to the writing of haiku verses, those brief, seventeen-syllable story-poems about things seen at the moment. They may, for example, preserve in words the flight of a butterfly or falling raindrops or breaking waves or passing clouds. They are "meditations . . . starting points for trains of thought."* Haiku verses invite the reader to accompany the writer, to experience mentally a brief event and to ponder its truth later.

*The Classic Tradition of Haiku, edited by Faubion Bowers; Dover Publications; Mineola, New York (1996).

Winter's Day (haiku)

A gray winter sky;

gray waves on an ebbing sea;

gray gulls in gray mist.

*A*n unknown author expressed a common yearning, "The human spirit needs places where nature has not been rearranged by the hand of man." Although it is difficult these days to find such a place in this populous world, I suggest we consider the sea as one of the last frontiers. Civilization stops at the shoreline, beyond which the sea is nature at its wildest. Beneath the surface, creatures now move virtually unchanged from the early Paleozoic Era.

There are those who compare
these daily paragraphs to
haiku, that popular Japanese
poetry form. There may be some similarity.
I present to the reader in less than a hundred
words a snapshot of the beach, a word picture
of a commonplace event, hopefully evoking a
response from the reader to continue thinking
about the subject. In my case, the writer simply points to a thing which interests him, invit-
ing the reader to consider it further.

*T*he little ark seashell, picked up this morning, is covered with dark, brown periostracum, a fibrous layer, protecting and camouflaging the top valve. When the unattractive covering is partially scraped away, a pearly white shell underneath is revealed, its radial ridges glistening in the sunshine. Are there not some people whom we know like this, too, crusty and forbidding at first glance, but actually kind and pleasing beneath a rough exterior?

The shapely, visually pleasing, silhouette of a cormorant perched on an offshore post is an arresting sight, as the eastern horizon brightens at daybreak. Its sensuous form—a long neck and slightly uplifted head and bill—gives one the feel of the Orient, a classic presence painted on silk, more an icon of the Far East than a shorebird of the Gulf of Mexico. Awaiting dawn, the cormorant now drops into the sea to begin a day of underwater fishing.

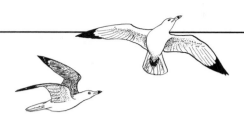

"All movement is to invisible music . . . although only a few people hear it," once wrote the artist Walter Anderson. Today one senses the music in the cadence of a gull's flapping wings. And it is found too in the frenetic pace of small sandpipers walking rapidly on the wet sand. "It is like part of a great symphony," and if we listen, we become part of the music instead of interruption, he concluded.* Such is the beach's melody.

*Quoted in *Fortune's Favorite Child: The Uneasy Life of Walter Anderson* by Christopher Maurer; University Press of Mississippi (2003).

A friend asks, "Why do you write the newspaper column?" After a moment to consider,
I respond, "For me it is an opportunity to
celebrate ordinary things, not calling attention
to the unusual or the spectacular, but defining
beauty in commonplace objects—a grain of
sand, a wave, wildflowers, a gull's flight.
Yet if I excluded the divine character of nature
that is God's creation, then these paragraphs
would be empty of truth."

*O*nce on a New England coast the poet Mary Oliver watched great blue herons just as we do today. She described one as "an old Chinese poet hunched in the white gown of his wings." Another she called "a blue preacher, flying in slow motion."* The two herons on our beach—Tweedledum and Tweedledee—stand in shallow water patiently fishing, as they do each day, their bluish plumage contrasting with a green sea and a gray sky.

*"Some Herons" by Mary Oliver; *New and Selected Poems*; Beacon Press, Boston (1992).

The list of the seven wonders of the ancient world was compiled in the second century B.C., all impressive structures built by man. But there are other wonders, common things that inspire our thoughts and senses, that lie close at hand. For instance, a piece of driftwood, untouched by human hands, lies on the wrack line this morning, carved by waves and wind, scarred by stones. It bears certain resemblance to a dolphin, a true wonder.

Pointing to the sparkling sea, a little girl said, "Mama, look at all the diamonds in the water." The sun's rays strike rippling  *waves this morning, illuminating a brilliant path from the viewer southward to the sun itself. Lovers through the ages have noted similar pathways of jewels, leading to full moons, shining above the sea. But it took a child's simplicity to correctly identify "diamonds" in a gleaming sea.*

In 1717 George Frederic Handel wrote his famous Water Music *to be played on a barge bearing King George I to a festive party. So popular was the presentation that the king ordered it to be played three times during the trip on the Thames. Now nearly three hundred years later, through the magic of a compact disk player and earphones, I listen to Handel's* Water Music *while strolling along the shore this cool, sunny, winter afternoon.*

Among the many interesting birds that grace our beaches, one, always pleasing to observe, is the belted kingfisher. Strictly construed, it is not a shorebird, because kingfishers reside inland too and indeed worldwide. On this cold, winter morning it is pure joy to observe the solitary little bird, sitting on the handrail of a footbridge, patiently awaiting a minnow to swim below. Then with a rattling cry, it dives into the water.

A belted kingfisher perches on a utility wire, looking downward onto a flat, calm, blue sea. Edward Howe Forbush described "this wild, grotesque, tousled-headed bird."* A superb fisherman, the kingfisher is endowed with the patience of Job, as it waits for prey to swim into view. The kingfisher's scientific name is derived from the word "halcyon," a fabled Greek bird with an ability to calm both winds and waves.*

**The Great House of Birds* edited by John Hay; Sierra Club Books, San Francisco (1996).

The blue sea lies before us today in all its winter beauty. Helen Keller once urged us to see things now as if we were to be stricken blind, to hear now as if stone deaf tomorrow, to touch as if we were to lose our tactile sense, to smell and taste as if we would lose those senses.* So it is today that we view the sea, hear breaking waves, touch grains of sand, taste a briny mist, and smell the sea wind's pungent odor.

*The Atlantic Online Website.

*W*ords to ponder: In her book, The Sense of Wonder, *Rachel Carson wrote, "Those who dwell among the beauties and mysteries of the earth are never alone or weary of life. . . . Those who contemplate the beauty of the earth find reserves of strength that will endure as long as life lasts. . . ."* The sunrise this morning brings with it a tranquility, sensed not only by the shorebirds, but also by those people who walk along the shore.*

*Quoted in Earth's Echo by Robert M. Hamma; Sorin Books; Notre Dame, Indiana (2002).

*A*s a score of seabirds occupy a sandbar today, I marvel at the miracle of migration. Although bird migration is best known, animals too migrate. Great herds of buffalo, whales, turtles, salmon, even lemmings travel great distances, not only because of climate, but perhaps to find a better food supply. In prehistoric times, man migrated seasonally to find a more friendly environment. Migration has fascinated the human mind for centuries. Writing about 625 B.C., Jeremiah the prophet observed, "Even the stork in the air knows its seasons; turtledove, swallow and thrush observe their time of return."*

*Jeremiah 8:7.

*A*s I enjoy a cup of tea this morning after a chilly beach walk, additional thoughts of tea come to mind. Those marvelous American clipper ships outsailed veteran fleets of Britain's East India Company, outsailing too England's Cutty Sark and others—a triumph of U.S. ingenuity! India, the world's biggest tea producer, will, I read, soon consume more tea than it grows. But East African countries, Kenya and Malawi, also grow choice leaves. The Irish  now surpass the English in tea consumption, more than eleven pounds per person annually. It was Jonathan Swift who concluded, tea is "water bewitched."*

*Quote by Jonathan Swift (1667–1745).

I find three sandburs stuck onto trousers, long unused, hanging in a closet. The bristly seeds, now pale with age, still retain sharp, pointed spines. In its wisdom, nature uses the sandbur's clinging ability to broadcast seeds. A Scottish ritual in the 1500s featured "a burry man," covered with sandburs, parading through town, visiting each house. People gave him gifts to fend off bad luck which had long been associated with burs.*

A Calendar of Forgotten English Words (2004) by Jeffery Kacirk.

A heron stands in shallow water, its head turned toward an approaching walker, its unblinking eyes calmly assessing the danger. What ancient wisdom of life lies behind those eyes? What collective memory is stored in its brain? From Paleocene times, the bird and its forebears have learned to survive. The heron waits and watches. Then, laboriously flying away to live another day, complaining loudly, it sounds a hoarse "braaak."

*T*he famous architect, Buckminster Fuller, thought that God should be considered a verb rather than a noun. God is the continual bestowing of love, the act of loving, he contended. On the beach today, God is in the warm sunshine, in the cool wind, in the inert sand, in the shore-birds, and in the rain—all his gifts, all his constant acts of giving. "Yes, God is a verb," Fuller wrote, always "reordering the universe."*

No More Secondhand God by Richard Buckminster Fuller.

*A*t water's edge today are clumps of gray clay, dredged up by waves from the depths of the sea. Archaeologists have found fragments of ancient clay pottery, some as old as 3,000 years, made by tribes that inhabited this beach long ago. Think of those early potters here, fashioning wet clay with their hands. The substance is basic to our very creation. Job addressed the Lord, "Remember now, you have made me as clay. . . ."

*Job 10:9.

The shell in my hand was once protection for a clam that had somehow through the ages learned to produce armor for survival. Its evolution is shrouded in mystery. "Today's evolutionists," C.S. Lewis wrote, "place man at the top of a staircase whose bottom steps are lost in obscurity. Medieval man thought that he was on the bottom step, looking upward toward the top, invisible in brilliant light."* I find myself looking up, too.

*The Discarded Image by C.S. Lewis, Cambridge University Press (1994).

*N*ine brown pelicans in a line fly eastward in the early morning light only a few feet above the sea. I have had a lifelong love affair with pelicans, beginning long ago when they were plentiful. Later they were threatened with extinction by certain pesticides and disap- peared from these shores for many years. Ungainly and awkward on the water, they achieve beauty and grace aloft when flying, as they do now with their measured wingbeats.

*L*ong stalks of bamboo
have washed ashore during
the night hours. This morning they rest high on the
beach, carried there by
a tidal surge of
three-and-a-half
feet. One stalk is slender and pliable, bending
in an artfully curved arc when held. The poet,
David Solway,* writes about the native grass,
"Bamboo talks," it makes music with the wind,
"chatting with a little bird . . . or whispering to
itself; . . . sometimes it sings."

*"Bamboo" by David Solway; *The Atlantic,* October 2004 issue;
Boston.

$\mathcal{T}$he tree-lined profile of the barrier island, some nine miles offshore, is vividly visible this sunny afternoon. The author, James Michener, once called himself a "nesomaniac," (a person madly in love with islands).* Other writers have similarly diagnosed themselves, Melville and Robert Louis Stevenson, to name but two. There is something appealing about islands, floating nebulously on dream-like seas, remote jewels beyond our grasp.

Mad About Islands by A. Grove Day; Mutual Publishing Co., Honolulu (1987).

The lighthouses on the barrier islands were essential in the early days to warn sailing ships, not only of the islands themselves, but also of dangerous shoals and very shallow water. Consider the lightkeeper's lonely life on the north tip of Chandeleur. Although living in a virtual paradise, he had long years of solitude, daily tending the light, polishing the lens, refueling the wick, and viewing distant ships sailing by.

Today is a cloudy, cool day on the beach,
overcast, gray and somber. For centuries,
before clouds were identified as water vapor
and classified into types—cirrus, cumulus and
stratus—people called them "essences."
The word refers to things ephemeral, distilled
and spiritual. And so it is today that we watch
"essences" as they float seaward, silently and
gracefully, driven by the north wind, replaced
overhead at once by other clouds in endless
procession.

A pecan tree near the beach road is home to a large family of squirrels. Having observed them for years, I find them to be graceful, alert, smart animals. Some people reject them as rodents, which of course they are. But they intelligently save nuts to eat the remainder of the year, although they sometimes forget where they are hidden. Occasionally when I am out of town in autumn, they fill my beach-walking shoes with pecans.

In a clear, early morning, blue sky, two artificial clouds have appeared. They are contrails from the exhausts of high-flying jet airplanes five miles or more above the coastline.
The engines' exhausts contain moisture that vaporizes in the cold air, causing condensation. The higher of the contrails retains its shape for

nearly an hour, but the lower one disperses, giving every appearance now of a normal, altocumulus cloud.

A fully ebbed tide has exposed large numbers of seashells, normally covered by water. Upon examination, one sees that small holes have been bored into most of the shells—the work of oyster drills, predatory snails, archenemies of shellfish. An exception appears to be clams, their heavy, chalky shells apparently too thick for drills to penetrate. All the other shells, like the arks, tellins and cockles, bear telltale holes, evidence of fatal oyster drill attacks.

*M*oon-whitened waves roll in tonight from the dark expanse of the sea. Breaking on shore, the waves make a rushing noise, as frothy water rushes back into the sea. It is a hymn of creation, a sound repeated through the eons, a sound that reminds one of other countless beaches upon which waves have come ashore, a  sound heard and understood by legions of creatures—shorebirds, fish, all sealife and people like us.

$\mathcal{M}$oon jellyfish are rarely seen on our beach in winter. Yet six of them are stranded in a low tide this cold January morning. The saucer-shaped jellies measure about ten inches in diameter, all resting on dry sandbars. Hardy enough to survive beachings, they are alive, responding to a touch by quivering their translucent bodies. Surely the next tide will bear them away to the safety of deep water. In the meantime, they wait patiently.

*S*ilence is one of a beach walk's many gifts. Only faint sounds from a faraway locomotive and a muted din from the beach road are heard today. Except for the cries of shorebirds and the babble of wavelets—acceptable natural sounds—there is peaceful silence. Kierkegaard* wrote that if he were a doctor and could prescribe one remedy for modern man it would be silence. Today's walk is a brief respite from the world's clamor.

*Soren Kierkegaard (1813–1855), philosopher.

*W*alt Whitman had a lasting memory of beaches of which he often wrote. In 1855 he remembered a beach similar to the one we walk today. "The hurrying tumbling waves and quickbroken crests . . . the strata of col-ored clouds . . . the horizon's edge, the flying

seacrow,* . . . the fragrance of saltmarsh and shoremud . . ."** —all became a part of him when he was a child, just as our beach becomes an inseparable piece of us.

*Probably a fishcrow.
**Leaves of Grass by Walt Whitman.

In the 1940s the artist Walter Anderson rowed his ten-foot skiff from our coast some thirty-odd miles to North Island in the Chandeleurs, spending three weeks observing pelicans in the huge rookery there. It is said that he so identified himself with the birds that he mentally became a pelican. It was there that he composed a dictionary of their sounds. And it was there too where he drew hundreds of pelican sketches.*

*Illustration courtesy of the Anderson family and the Walter Anderson Museum of Art, Ocean Springs, Mississippi.

Cold weather decreases activity all along the beach by shorebirds and humans alike. Most shorebirds have flown away to the small craft harbor, escaping the chill of the north wind. Other humans with better judgment than I remain comfortable indoors. I miss my daily encounters in past seasons with the little kingfisher who faithfully stayed on his perch every daylight hour of even the coldest of days despite the absence of other shorebirds.

*T*homas Merton wrote that everyone should
have some place, "some corner where
no one will find you or notice you," a place
"to untether yourself from the world . . .
loosing all the fine strings and strands of
tension that bind you . . . to the presence of
other men."* At certain times, especially in

autumn and winter when
it is thinly populated,
our beach provides such
solitude, a place set apart
for a person to seek
peace and tranquility.

*A Book of Hours by Thomas Merton, edited by Kathleen Deignan;
Sorin Books, Notre Dame, Indiana (2006).

The Beach in
Spring

*S*itting on the seawall, prepared to think about things such as life and death, I find my mind diverted to little yellow flowers growing nearby. Happy little blooms, they bob in the gusting sea wind, sending a message of beauty to anyone who may glance their way. Their role in life is to exist but a few days, growing in arid sand, praising their Creator, giving joy to all who view them and to other people who may read these sentences, flowers unseen.

$\mathcal{O}$n beach walks there are spread before us expansive seascapes that we scan daily, noting with care incoming waves and scudding clouds. We also look intently for seashells and driftwood, but pay scant attention to our interior landscapes, those places where our minds and souls reside. Neglecting to tend the interior spaces, we abandon the important and choose the transitory. Visit those interior landscapes occasionally. So begins an exploration of self.

Watching a willet wade in the shallows is seeing poetry in motion. Our largest sandpiper, an indus-trious, graceful shorebird, the willet is solidly gray until it takes flight, then displays flashing-ly exciting, black-and-white wings. Its name comes from the piercing, shrill cry of alarm as it flies away, "will-will-it." "Chevalier" is the bird's apt name in French, and "Playero" in Spanish—both far more idyllic and lyrical than its English moniker.

*A*t dawn, the sea is flatly calm, mirror-like, without discernible movement, although we know that the morning's tide is already at work. Distantly, a wind stirs, spoiling the smoothness in a patch or two. In his poem, "East Coker," T.S. Eliot wrote, "Out at sea the dawn wind wrinkles and slides."* It is an apt description of what is happening, the "wrinkling" of the sea, little wavelets, announcing that the night watch has ended.

*"East Coker," *Four Quartets,* by T.S. Eliot; Harcourt, Brace, Jovanovich; New York (1971).

*T*here is a profound relationship between walking and thinking, walking and culture, say reviewers of Rebecca Solnit's book, Wanderlust.* The author points to the need for making time and space for walking in an automobile-dependent world. Among famous walkers, she cites Coleridge, Wordsworth, Keats, Rousseau and many others who depended on walks for inspiration. We too know about the mental stimulation of walks by the sea.

*Wanderlust: A History of Walking by Rebecca Solnit; Viking, New York (2000).

*B*eautiful camellias are blooming all along the beach road in bedraggled gardens by vacant lots where handsome homes once stood. My father  planted many small camellia bushes in the 1940s, some of which have become trees. Each flower, I tell my grandchildren, is a message of love from my long-deceased father. It is remarkable that even the more severely damaged plants are now producing perfectly formed, healthy blossoms.

White-capped waves roll shoreward this morning. In seemingly endless procession, they are spaced in five-second intervals, twelve crashing waves every minute. It is the tempo of the sea, the earth's natural measurement of time, a rhythm established long before man considered clocks or calendars. The cadence of waves, the rise and fall of the sea, sunrises and sunsets, orbiting stars, even the pulsating wind—all are nature's metronomes.

The sea is far too rough and windy today for
black skimmers to fish as they would normally,
flying inches above the water, their mandibles
slicing the surface. Their preference is a calm
sea, which occurs most frequently at dawn
and after sunset. Yet at mid-morning a flight
of six skimmers flies gracefully above the
shoreline, first eastward and then returning.
Surely, it could only be the sheer joy of flight
that propels them into gale-force winds.

The wind blows heavily today in violent gusts, causing the trees beside the beach road to roil in response. Even the leafless ones, like sycamores and pecans, offering the least resistance to the gale, bend, intoning a whistling sound. With leafed limbs, the oaks move erratically, audibly whispering. Each tree has its own wind-given voice. The bedazzling purple blooms of the Japanese magnolia flutter and dance on leafless branches.

There are so few people walking on the beach these days that for weeks my footprints were the only ones, but today others have appeared, those of a barefooted man and a dog. My curiosity reminds me of Robinson Crusoe's when he first saw Friday's footsteps in the sand of their desert island. My predecessor's footprints are mostly at water's edge, but from time to time stray away toward interesting bits of driftwood, shells and debris.

The whelk shell, lying at water's edge this morning, is so commonplace that it is usually ignored by beach walkers. Yet, on close inspection, its architecture, graceful spirals and whorls, displays an artful masterpiece. Growth ridges on the shell's exterior are too numerous to count. The little, whelkish snail that originally occupied the shell is long gone, but perhaps now a hermit crab will discover that the empty carapace is a suitable habitat.

Sometimes on beach walks, I carry a compact magnifying glass; its ten-power strength makes it a fascinating tool. A clump of brown gulfweed, also called sargassum, *is transformed under the lens. Seen by unaided eyes, it is a maze of tangled limbs, an almost unidentifiable mass, but magnified, it becomes wonderfully defined, with a trunk, branches and berries. Also revealed are live creatures, small crustaceans, clinging to its tan limbs.*

*T*he fishermen on the public pier this morning
and those along the shore—casting both live
and artificial bait, wading hip-deep, talking
happily to one another, comparing fish—
are all convivial, contented and in good humor.
Fishermen are generally affable. Are they not
of the same kind of people who populate
Izaak Walton's book, The Compleat Angler,
written in 1653, and those "happy, simple
fisherfolk" who "cast their nets in Galilee"?*

*"They cast their nets in Galilee," by William Alexander Percy,
Greenville, Mississippi (1924).

There is much similarity in the male animal, whether he be avian or human. A case in point is the behavior of male gulls on the beach this morning. At the height of the courtship season now their plumage is stark black and shining white, striking colors. Their intense behavior indicates a high metabolism. Strutting and preening, the male gulls are flamboyant, not unlike the boys down the beach trying to impress nearby girls.

*S*horebirds are mating earlier than usual this year. The pairing and selection of mates is already underway for laughing gulls. From a distance I observe a courtship. Separating themselves from the flock, a male and female gull stand together, both facing the sea. Then ensues a vocal duet. Each bird in turn, lifting its bill skyward, emits a pleasant, cooing sound. It is part of their courtship ritual, a time-honored spring-time ceremony.

$\mathcal{A}$ horseshoe crab, burrowing into the wet sand to lay her eggs, may have traveled as many as twenty miles for this appointment with destiny. She brings with her two smaller males to fertilize the eggs. There is much about nature that we do not know, such as the mystical timing of this event. How can these dumb creatures, living far away, guided by tides and phases of the moon, arrive here unaided to perform the ageless act of procreation?

*W*atching a least tern through binoculars this morning, I see the male bring a silver minnow to its mate, a generous gift authenticating their pairing, a symbol of courtship. The practice is similar, is it not, to that found in human romances where a gift seals a relationship? In the nest are two spotted eggs that will hatch in three weeks. After emerging from the shells, the nestlings will begin flying four weeks later.*

*The Audubon Society Encyclopedia of North American Birds by John K. Terres; Alfred A. Knopf, New York (1980).

*S*ome wonderful words have disappeared from the English language: "Hurrocks," the murmuring sound as the sea surges ashore. "Rack," a body of clouds driven by the wind. "Toshers," people who walk along a shore hunting valuables. "Venters," anything which the wind or tide washes onto the beach. A "fardel," a quantity of valueless things, like a collection of broken seashells. A "Hobbes's voyage," a leap into the dark, a dubious venture.*

A Calendar of Forgotten English Words by Jeffery Kacirk (2004).

*A*n unwritten law for beachwalkers is "Never disturb a sand castle that someone has built on the beach." Today there is an elaborate labyrinth of passages and moats, towering turrets and walls all carefully molded in sand. Located at water's edge, the castle will soon be consumed by incoming waves and wind. Another sculpture, that of a prone man sleeping on the beach, will meet the same fate as waves are already erasing the sandman's feet.

*I*t is said that one day Saint Francis was joyfully walking through a town, asking its people to sing along with him. Upon coming to a bare almond tree, he addressed it, "Brother Almond, speak to me of God." Immediately the tree was covered with blossoms.* Perhaps the spirit of the saint spoke to the two trees growing near the beach road, because only a few days ago they were barren, and today they are in full bloom.

Through the Year with Francis of Assisi by Murray Bodo; Doubleday & Company, Inc., New York (1987).

*R*oosting today on exposed sandbars along with a motley group of gulls, terns and pelicans are several black skimmers. Fascinating birds, they have much longer, lower beaks than upper ones. When skimmers are feeding, their lower beak slices the surface of the water, catching small fish and bits of sea life. Sometimes they fish in daylight, but their preference is at dusk and after nightfall when the sea is calmer.

The number of plovers on the beach this mid-April morning is less than last month, many having already migrated to the Arctic. Two on the sand flats only a short distance away speak to each other in melodic tones, actually a plaintive whistling. It is said that of all shorebirds the call of the plover is most similar to the human voice. Today their calls are cello-like, expressions heard sometimes in Johannes Brahms' sonatas.

*F*or many years now, I have fallen into the daily practice of addressing great blue herons, as they stand silently in the flats. A stranger might think this old man is addled to say "Good morning!" to birds; but after all, we are more than passing acquaintances. The herons are my long-standing friends. What bad things might the birds think if I were to ignore them? The herons respond to my greeting with a simple, pleasant nod of their heads.

*S*omeone forgot to tell the shorebirds that daylight-saving time went into effect last night, because at sunrise, their usual hour of awaking, here they are noisily searching for food. The sham of changing clocks, the artificiality of it, is an absurd practice. Does one think for a moment that the universe is a whit different? Do the tides alter their rising and falling? Is the moon's orbit corrected? Will fruit ripen an hour sooner?

A walk along the shoreline separates one from his normal routine. He becomes immersed in a different world, one in which time is measured, not by a clock, but by other things—the cadence of waves, grains of sand slipping through fingers, the measured beats of a gull's wings. It is then that one is more attuned to the present, a realization that this is the way things actually are and the way they have been since the very beginning.

*F*inding three beige-colored eggs in a depression in the sand is a discovery that fills the heart with joy. Encased within the fragile shells is new life. What is happening in there now? What mystical force is at work, transforming yolk and albumen into living creatures who will mature and leave the shells in a few days? Whether they will be gulls or skimmers, who knows? But the alchemy of creation is at work at this moment.

Consider for a moment the subject of leadership among beach creatures. A line of nine brown pelicans flies eastward above the shore. Eight birds follow one leader, obeying his every command to veer left or right. Near the seawall, a colony of ants seems to be of one mind, with each insect performing its assigned task. Neither pelicans nor ants question (as far as we know) their leaders' commands. All obey implicitly.

The shorebirds have discovered a cache of horseshoe crab eggs at water's edge this morning. For them it has become a jubilee gathering! Feasting on the eggs are sanderlings, turnstones, plovers and a few willets. Punctured by the pecking of their bills, the wet sand records each penetration. Of all the birds, the willets are most favored because their long bills allow them to probe deeper into the sand than the short-billed birds.

"*The* most precious things of life are near at hand," wrote John Burroughs, "without money and without price."* And so they are. Consider, for instance, this morning's sunrise or the expanse of sea before us or the feel of the southerly breeze or the procession of clouds overhead or the shorebirds feeding peacefully in the shallows or the crunch of white sand underfoot. All are precious things, treasures without price, gifts to enjoy.

**John Burroughs' America*; Dover Publications; Mineola, New York (1997).

A flock of starlings, numbering a hundred or more birds, wheels over the beach road and lands on the sand. Many insist that starlings are pests, but allow me to give you a minority opinion. They are in fact very attractive birds. At first glance they may appear black, but on closer inspection you will find them to be glossy purple, displaying lustrous, rainbow-like colors. And now in spring their bills have become a lemony yellow color.

*Y*esterday's starlings
(little stars) have
returned to the
beach again today in
even greater num-
bers, nearly 200 now
by count. They are preparing, one guesses,
for their migrating flight northward. It is difficult to believe that the species had its beginning on this hemisphere when 100 of the
birds were released in New York's Central Park
in 1890. Now perhaps the most numerous of
all American birds, starlings have multiplied
ceaselessly.

A heron feather lying at water's edge this morning is one of nature's most remarkable creations. Not only does it aid in flight, it also insulates and protects the bird from rain. Feathers are keratin, the same stuff of which horns, hoofs, bills, and indeed our own fingernails are made. The intricacy of a feather's design is amazing. From the shaft grow a hundred filaments and from each filament grow a hundred more downy strands.

The top of a submerged tree branch is revealed briefly in the troughs between measured swells this morning, seen for a moment then covered by the rise of the next swell. When visible, a portion of the branch looks as if it were a demon, a creature of the sea, dragon-like in appearance. Although stationary, the apparition appears to be moving in the swells. Could it be that "Nessie," the Loch Ness monster, had a similar beginning?

The cockle shell found
this morning at water's edge
deserves close scrutiny, because of the
symmetrical beauty of its radial ridges. Only
two inches wide, the shell has twenty-eight
ribs on the exterior of the top valve, so deeply
and expertly sculptured that the pattern of
etched lines becomes an intricate work of art.
Is it possible for a person to fully comprehend
its magnificent geometry and then to deny the
existence of God?

In warm months it is the practice of stingrays to approach the shoreline, lying there without moving. Normally they occupy depressions in deeper water. For years we had wondered why they moved so near the shore. Today the question has been answered. They come near shore to feast on small minnows that flourish there in great numbers when temperatures climb. We watched this morning as a stingray ambushed a school of minnows.

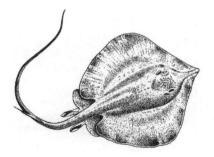

A pacific sea lying before us this afternoon is far removed from the one that assaulted this beach in 2005. In earlier years, such tempests

NASA PHOTO

were given descriptive names, such as "the 1947 hurricane." Later, as Dery Bennett reminds us, they were given fish names— alefish, eel, bass, carp, etc.* After which came invertebrate names—abalone, clam, barnacle, etc. Then came a string of people's names and, finally, Katrina, one not soon to be forgotten.

*Dery Bennett, editor, *Underwater Naturalist*, Vol. 27, No. 3 Bulletin of the American Littoral Society, Sandy Hook, Highlands, New Jersey.

A new moon is seen tonight from the beach through moving clouds, visible for a few moments, then disappearing behind advancing clouds. The British poet, Alfred Noyes, described a similar scene: "The moon was a ghostly galleon tossed upon cloudy seas. . . ."*

Given a sense of motion by the passing clouds, the horned moon does indeed resemble a sea craft with a distinct bow and stern, navigating in turbulent weather.

*"The Highwayman" by Alfred Noyes (1880–1958).

The handsome
ketch sailing
offshore under
full sail is equipped
with the most advanced
navigational system, pinpointing its
position from satellites. But consider those
early helmsmen who set courses even before
the compass was invented about 1280 A.D.
They were guided by stars at night and the
sun by day. On cloudy days they sailed only by
dead reckoning unaided by celestial bodies.
Yet they crossed distant oceans and found
their ports.

Illustration: The Davis quadrant, a navigation instrument invented by
Captain John Davis in 1594.

This is the season for dragonflies, and they
will be with us until autumn. Darners, so
named because they resemble darning needles, abound this morning in the grassy mar-
gins of the beach road. Because people do
not darn these days, few will have even seen a
darning needle. Sometimes called "mosquito
hawks," darners dine on all insects. This
morning a dozen or so
fly above a weed patch
in hot pursuit of gnats
and shoreflies.

A mist falls on the
beach this morning,
very fine droplets,
slanting in their
descent in a mild
south breeze.
Although not rain,
the mist dampens

face, hand and clothes, falling softly on the
sand, leaving no craters as do raindrops.
It lessens visibility, but not like opaque fog.
Sandburg wrote of "the beauty of mist . . .
pearl and gray" and how it changes drab
scenes "into points of interest quivering with
color."*

*"Last Answers," *The Complete Poems of Carl Sandburg*; Harcourt
Brace Jovanovich, Inc., New York (1970).

*W*hen the upper valve of an oyster shell was found this morning at water's edge, it reflected an array of colors from a mother-of-pearl interior—blues, pinks and greens. Glittering prisms danced in the bright sunlight. Taken home, the shell lost its luminous luster. Gone were the delicate colors. All that remained was a drab, gray oyster shell. It would have been wiser to have left it at water's edge, lying in the beauty of its own milieu.

*S*horebirds feed differently. Terns dive vertically into the sea to capture small minnows. Other diving birds are brown pelicans and ospreys, often pursuing larger prey. Swooping low, gulls forage for floating food and scavenge along the shoreline. Some ducks, loons and cormorants submerge to hunt for their sustenance. Skimmers are surface fishers. Willets, plovers, peeps and their ilk find food at water's edge and in the shallows.

$\mathcal{A}$t water's edge this morning lies a top valve of a small scallop shell; perfectly preserved, it was sculpted without scars or other flaws, pure artistry. A bay scallop, this one is called. Through the ages, poets and painters have recorded the scallop's beauty and symmetry. Pompeii's buildings were adorned with scallop art. Appearing in heraldry, scallop shells turn up in the coats of arms of Winston Churchill, John Wesley and Pope Benedict XVI.

*T*he scallop shell found earlier captures my attention, not only for its marked artistry of design, but also for other reasons. I count its concentric rings or ridges. It is said that scallops live as long as eighteen years, each year visible in a sequence of markings, called the annuli. Related to oysters, scallops are more mobile, swimming freely in the sea by opening and closing their shells. Inside, the shell is pearly white, having a soft, satiny feel to the touch.

A yellow wildflower
with eight delicate petals
grows by the seawall.
Each day I stop to say
hello and ask how it fares.
Today, a brisk sea wind moves the petals in a tremor of sorts. The flower's identity is uncertain. Perhaps it is a type of dandelion or maybe a kind of golden aster. But does its lack of identity make it any less beautiful to us? "What's in a name? That which we call a rose by any other name would smell as sweet," Shakespeare wrote.*

Romeo and Juliet by William Shakespeare.

A danger in beach walking these days is a possible attack by least terns. If the little birds perceive that their nests are threatened in any way, they will dive fearlessly on the supposed offender, be it human, canine, or tractor. Occasionally a walker sustains a painful scalp wound from a diving tern. Although we carefully avoid their nests, we carry with us a simple defense, a thin bamboo joint held overhead to fend off possible attacks.

It is possible to gauge the time that drift-wood has been floating in the sea by the number of barnacles that it has acquired. A piece of wood found at water's edge today has only three small, acorn barnacles, while another is so encrusted with shells that the entire surface of the wood itself is covered. Another indicator is the size of the barnacles. Small shells, only brief flotation; large adult shells tell of the driftwood's long seaborne journey.

*N*ature arms its wild creatures with camou-
flage, an art of disguising to deceive both
enemy and prey. The coloration of the
stingray lying at water's edge today is deceiv-
ing. Its top side blends with the color of the
wet sand on which it rests. An osprey flying
overhead above the ray will not spot it
easily, nor will minnows swimming nearby. In addition,
the stingray has now bur-
rowed itself under the
sand, camouflaging itself
completely.

*N*ine months ago the hurricane uprooted trees, leaving them submerged in the shallows. There they remain. The scene reminds one of Whitman's poem. "The world below the brine," he wrote, "forests at the bottom of the sea—the branches and leaves, sea-lettuce, vast lichens, strange flowers and seeds—the thick tangle, openings, and pink turf, different colors, pale gray and green, purple, white and gold—the play of light through the water . . . ."

*"The World Below the Brine" by Walt Whitman; *American Poetry*; The Library of America; New York (1984).

*S*andpipers dominate the beach at water's edge this morning. Many members of the sandpiper family—dowitchers, dunlins, godwits, knots, sanderlings, stilts, snipes, turnstones, willets and yellow-legs— have visited our beach in recent weeks. The poet, Carl Sandburg, wrote about their presence, "the script of their feet . . ." is written in the morning, ". . . gone at noon," erased by the incoming tide.* But some will be there again tomorrow, writing once again.

*"Sandpipers," *The Complete Poems of Carl Sandburg*; Harcourt Brace Jovanovich, Inc., New York (1970).

"*Bring me the sunset in a cup . . . ,*" once wrote Emily Dickinson in a poem.* And I too would like to preserve the beauty of today's sunset so that it might be savored properly on dark, rainy days or at some hour of need. Nearing its northern journey, the sun is a red ball, now partially below the western horizon, its rays reaching high into the sky, illuminating clouds in brilliant colors—pinks, oranges, reds—a scene to be saved in memory.

*"Bring me the sunset in a cup," *American Poetry*; The Library of America; New York (1984).

The Beach in
Summer

The arrival of the
first whelk egg case
each summer is another indication of renewal
of life on the beach, a reminder that regenera-
tion is at work here once again. Empty of
eggs now, the long capsule looks like a string
of amber poker chips, attractive enough to be
worn as a necklace. Awash in the sea, an egg
will mature and grow a remarkably complex,
left-handed shell. The finely shaped, spiral
sculpture becomes nature's work of art.

A wildflower sadly missed this summer is the beautiful white morning glory that in past years graced our beach every summer day. We look in vain for their emergence from the barren sand in which they had prospered in earlier seasons. The famed Mississippi novelist, Richard Wright, who in his declining years penned nothing but haiku verse, once wrote, "A little girl stares, dewy eyes round with wonder, at morning glories."*

Haiku: The Other World by Richard Wright; Random House, Inc., New York (1998).

*E*arly in the morning my elongated shadow stretches far to the west with the sun at my back. Although after awhile, as the sun rises higher, the shortened shadow still frightens roosting gulls into flight. Moving shadows awaken within birds' collective memories the alarm of predators attacking. Their instinct is to flee, even though it may be only a harmless umbra. Yet it is wiser to fly away, because one day such a shadow may be from an osprey.

A late-afternoon drama on the beach unfolds: A single, large herring gull raids a least tern nest, inciting the ire, not only of its two occupants, but also of the entire least tern neighborhood. Seven of the feisty little birds attack the gull furiously, screeching, "Zeeek! zeeek! zeeek!" At last sight, the gull was in full retreat, pursued by seven terns. Having saved the nest, the birds return victorious to settle on their sandy nests in the stillness of the evening.

*T*ypical of summer days, the southern horizon is banked with cumulus clouds. Cumulus is a Latin word translated "a heap," aptly describing today's accumulation of clouds. On the sea, their shadows darken patches of water; some dark blue, others lighter in color. A mild, southerly wind brings the clouds over the mainland. "How softly runs the afternoon," wrote Charles Hanson Towne, "beneath the billowy clouds of June. . . ."*

*"How Softly Runs the Afternoon," a poem by Charles Hanson Towne (1877–1949).

Summer is the season to watch hermit crabs, earning their name because of their solitary behavior. Living in shells vacated by various gastropods, hermits live alone. Even when a small hermit occupies a very large shell, he never shares it with a mate. Then, it might well be asked, "How does the species propagate?" This morning, we witnessed one hermit in pursuit of another in the shallows, both scurrying along carrying burdensome shells.

*T*he magical presence of three American oystercatchers has transformed the beach today. The other shorebirds acknowledge the newcomers. Plovers and peeps stop their feeding at water's edge, watching warily; a flock of gulls roosting nearby edges away from the big, black-and-white birds with their large, red bills. The new arrivals' bills are strong, knife-like instruments, fully capable of opening oyster and clam shells.

Life's simple pleasures enlighten the day. A seashell found at water's edge is surely not grand enough for a serious collector to keep, but it has its attributes, a smooth, shapely exterior and a pearl-like interior. Standing atop a post, a gull is not a specimen to be recorded in a birdwatcher's journal, but it is a pleasing bird to watch for a while. Finding it entertaining to look at such commonplace things, discovering their innate charm, is a blessing.

The beach has lessons to teach us, if we are open to its instruction. Today's wisdom, I think, is to be patient. Few things along the shoreline are hurried. On an offshore post sits a gull, passively awaiting an incoming tide, which slowly inches up the sand beach. Nothing hastens its rise. Pulled by moon and sun, the tide moves at its own pace in sync with those heavenly bodies. If the gull knows to wait for high tide, then we must also learn to wait.

A dappled sea lies before us this morning, beneath a dappled sky. A number of low-level clouds, scudding northward, mottle the sea, marking the water with their moving shadows. The sand, too, is mottled with the clouds' slowly moving umbras. "Glory be to God for dappled things," wrote Gerard Manley Hopkins, "for skies of couple-color, for . . . stipple upon trout that swim, . . . whatever is fickle, freckled (who knows how?) . . . ."*

*"Pied Beauty" by Gerard Manley Hopkins; *A Selection of His Poems,* edited by W.H. Gardner; Penguin Books, Baltimore (1956).

*P*uffy, summer-like, downy clouds drift lazily overhead, slowly finding their way northward in gentle breezes. Who else sees these clouds? Young lovers looking upward from a grassy field? An old woman peering out her bedroom window? A prisoner gazing at them through bars? A businessman walking down the street? Perhaps another beachwalker? But how many countless others do not see them at all, never once looking skyward?

Beachwalkers experience a sense of expectancy. What gift has the sea brought us today? When the day's tide is high and when waves come rolling ashore, there are more gifts than on calmer days. Today's bounty includes two puffers, several shells, three bits of driftwood, and two hawsers from ships. It is not so much the item itself that fascinates me, but rather to hold and feel each one and to contemplate its journey to this beach.

Surprisingly our beach morning glories have returned! Two magnificent, white blooms with yellow throats have opened this morning not far from the sandy patch where they had grown in profusion in recent years. A month before the hurricane, tractors had buried all the plants while building a concrete boat launching ramp. We thought then that the morning glories had been destroyed forever. Now miraculously at least one plant has survived!

*I*n Japan, morning glories are called "asagao,"
combining their words "asa," translated
"morning," and "gao," meaning "face." So it
is that today we look at their blooms, their
"morning faces," lifted sunward. It is said that
the flowers last only one day, a brief span of
life. Indeed, sometimes they close their petals
finally at noon, having absorbed a sufficiency
of sunlight. We mourn their demise, but celebrate their fragile beauty, even if we enjoy it
but fleetingly.

*F*ootprints on the beach this afternoon tell us
that hundreds of gulls, terns and skimmers
had gathered at this spot earlier in the day.
Some impressions in the sand are blurred,
tracks on top of tracks, others erased when
the birds walked away. This
is the season too when
large sea turtle
tracks appear on
our barrier islands,
leading to caches of
buried eggs. Leatherbacks, ridleys and greens
may travel a thousand miles to lay eggs on
those beaches.

A stingray, lying quietly but watchfully at water's edge this morning, is not a dangerous creature. At the slightest intrusion, it will flee to safety. Only when stepped upon or attacked by a predator does the ray whip its barbed tail in defense. The ray had partially buried itself in sand with only eyes and tail visible. Alarmed at our presence, "flying" through the water on its large pectoral wings, the graceful fish vanishes silently into the deep.

A noble bird has perished, its lifeless body at water's edge awash in the gentle waves. Great blue herons possess dignity, even in death. Although it is an end that we will all experience sooner or later, the reality of passing away is difficult to accept. Yesterday the stately heron was alive; today it is no more—nature's finality. For the heron, I make a simple cenotaph, a tall driftwood pole, pushed deep into the wet sand where the bird usually stood.

It is a lazy, summer afternoon with little activity on the beach. Gone are the morning fishermen, wading in the shallows. Gone too are the sunbathers who bared themselves to the mid-summer sun, departing at the noon hour. A quietness settles on the beach. Active all morning, shorebirds enjoy a siesta, dozing on the deserted shore. From the sand flats, a great blue heron rises on unhurried wing beats, flying toward the oaks across the beach road.

*A*t daybreak a flight of eight brown pelicans flies eastward in single file toward the rising sun. Ungainly, awkward birds on land and when floating on the surface, they attain majestic grace and beauty of movement when aloft. Watch them wing their way eastward for a while before wheeling toward the mainland and retracing their flight westward. Their performance, a daily event this month, is called "the dawn patrol" by beach walkers.

If our beach were a stage, what an outstanding cast we would have. In a starring role, a stately great blue heron stands in the shallows. Although its voice is seldom heard, the bird has a magnificent stage presence, one that a great actor could well emulate. In lesser, supporting roles are two snowy egrets, dancing on the flats. Now a flight of skimmers appears, their bills gracefully rippling the calm, still water, another fine theatrical performance.

*Y*esterday there was a wedding on the beach. At sunset, the couple, families, and friends gathered at the shoreline for the ceremony. Watched from afar, it was an enchanting scene. Could the couple have chosen a finer cathedral for their union? Narthex, nave, transepts, apse, altar—all were there in nature's most beautiful forms. Throughout their lives, the couple will carry with them memories of that blessed hour at the shore.

*I*f a man wants to be truly alone, Emerson once wrote, "let him look at the stars."* What magnificence there is in the night sky now, a

 canopy of celestial light! But so few people actually "see" nature, he observed. It is there before them continually every day, but seldom are even the most common things noted. How neglected is the beauty of this very night, unseen by people closeted in their houses and automobiles.

*Ralph Waldo Emerson, Essays and Lectures; The Library of America, New York (1983).

The tractor driver who
plowed the vegetation by the
seawall today was merely following orders,
I am certain, to get rid of the weeds growing
there. However, perhaps unknowingly, he
destroyed a patch of beautiful wildflowers, a
large expanse of colorful Indian Blankets,
asters, morning glories, and a number of blue
spiderworts. Gathering a few of the sheared
blooms, I am saddened at the loss, but know
the plants will soon grow back.

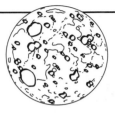

The high tide this morning is sometimes called a "spring tide." But the name has nothing to do with the season. Its earliest known use was in the 1500s and had to do with a tide "springing" or lifting a heavy sailing vessel so that it could leave a shallow harbor. Such tides occur a few days after full moons and are simply unusually high tides. Today's flood tide reaches far up the sand beach, disturbing a flock of roosting gulls.

The frequency of whitecaps today is one every three seconds. Yesterday there were no waves, just sweeping swells timed at intervals of ten seconds. Sea waves are different, much larger, and do not break until they encounter

a shore. Oceanographers study their height, troughs, etc., to determine where they originated. At Cape Town, South Africa, huge waves were identified that had begun thousands of miles away in Drake Passage at the tip of South America.

*T*here are new tracks in the sand on the beach this morning, not those left by shore-birds. They are the claw prints of fiddler crabs! Since the hurricane, nearly a year ago, we had not seen fiddlers, believing that they were victims of the storm and thereafter of the huge tractors in the beach cleanup. The good news is that the fiddlers have returned and in large numbers. We see one now, peering from its burrow, its slender eyestalks watching us intently.

*W*atch the shadow of an overhead cloud, cast first over the sea and then the sand beach, as it speeds on its northward journey. The word, shadow, is defined as absence of light. A book that I am reading is titled The Shadow of God, *an autobiography of Charles Scribner III,* who writes that light is indeed the shadow of God. He calls on Plato and Sir Thomas Browne to make the point. If he is correct, today's sunlight takes on new meaning.*

*The Shadow of God by Charles Scribner III; Doubleday, New York (2006).

A small jellyfish swims nicely
this morning in the calm sea.
Inflating and deflating its body
with water, the jelly moves from one point to
another, a major achievement for a creature
normally floating willy-nilly where wind and
current carry it. Swimming is the business of
the day for the jelly. But what about the
observer? Isn't it a waste of time to watch the
jellyfish? Surely there must be more important
things for me to do today. Maybe not.

This very month, two years ago prior to the hurricane, I counted over fifty morning glory blossoms at this particular spot on the beach. Last year only a few appeared at the very height of the wildflower season. But all that has changed! Today we tally more than eighty blooming morning glories, far more than in previous years! Gone is the despair that we felt for the beach, its plants and its creatures after the tempest. Restorative healing has occurred!

*Y*esterday cicadas noisily announced their presence in an oak tree by the beach road. Their staccato verses filled the night air, loud and grating to the ear. Christopher Morley rightly described the sound, "a chattering voltage like a broken wire."* Today I return to the tree to view the little insects at close range, but not one is seen. Hidden, I guess, under the tree's bark, they enjoy the last days of their thirteen-year life.

*Quote by Christopher Morley (1890–1957).

After sunset, but before dark, an old heron, having stood stoically in the shallow water of the sand flats all day, lifts itself on ponderous wings to fly away to a night roost. Translate, if you will, its hoarse, gruff croaks upon leaving the beach. "Not many fish today!" or "Boy, what hot weather!" or merely, "See you tomorrow." In flight, the large bird's head folds back onto its shoulders. Slow, even wing beats bear the heron to a nearby bayou.

Clumps of gulfweed are floating ashore this morning. Their stalks, leaves and berries look very much like vegetation, but the weed is in fact a brown algae. Although shorebirds do not eat the plant itself, they do devour the little creatures that inhabit it—tiny shrimp, crabs, plankton and others. Kept afloat by berry-like bladders, gulfweed is buoyant and can be seen near the surface as sea currents and wave action deposit it at water's edge.

*O*ften in summer, beach walkers find messages etched in the sand. Nearly all the texts tell us that "Suzy loves John" or maybe "J.T. + S.J." Today's is different. It reads, "Thank you, Lord!" One asks, for what is the writer grateful? For a perfect summer day, for a lover, for some remembered act of kindness, for the sea wind? Or perhaps our scribe is simply responding to Saint Paul's injunction to give thanks " . . . always and for everything. . . ."*

*Ephesians 5:20.

Two creatures are moving along the shore this morning—a hermit crab and a fiddler,

cousins of sorts, belong to the same kingdom, phylum, subphylum, class and order. In the course of their development, the two species have chosen different protection against predators. Fiddlers dig burrows in the sand, sometimes twenty inches deep, while hermit crabs find deserted shells in which to dwell, both defenses working quite well for each.

The sand on the beach this morning resembles the crater-pocked surface of the moon. Last night's windstorm brought down large raindrops that left their impressions, rounded impact marks, one after another in the wet sand. Looking closely at the resulting patterns, one sees, not only artistic designs in the sand that would bring credit to the noted artist, M.C. Escher, but also the results of raindrops falling exactly upon impact points of previous ones.

There are continual confrontations between gulls and fiddler crabs, with gulls aggressively pursuing the little creatures. A record of their meetings can often be found later in the sand,

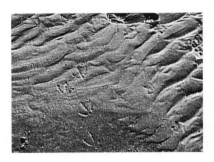

gulls' footprints alongside those of fiddlers. We can only guess at the drama of the encounter, wondering if the gull did in fact devour its victim, or did the fiddler reach its burrow in time? It is a matter of survival for the crab, requiring wily skill and good fortune.

*D*ark clouds of gnats, not the biting kind
but annoying midges, swarm at water's edge
this evening, attracted here, one guesses, by
decaying gulfweed washed ashore recently.
What pleasant thing can one write about
gnats? Not much. The poet, Keats, called
them a "wailful choir, . . . borne aloft or

sinking as the light
wind lives or dies."*
Perhaps their presence
here now is to
discourage people from
intruding upon a
nearby tern nesting area.

*"To Autumn" by John Keats; The New Oxford Book of English Verse; Oxford University Press (1972).

*P*icture this scene: Three least terns occupy a rude, sandy nest by the seawall, two adults and one fledgling. Barely able to fly, the young tern continually keeps its mouth open, expecting to be fed small minnows by the parent birds, as it had been since emerging from its shell. But the mother and father stoically ignore the fledgling's open mouth. Wise parents, they encourage the little bird to fish for itself, becoming independent of them.

*W*hen birds fly away at the approach of walkers, their flight illustrates a prime motive in the behavior, not only of shorebirds, but also of other creatures, including humans—self preservation. Deeply imbedded in all beings is the instinct to survive, to avoid death, to continue to live. It can be observed in jellyfish swimming away from danger, in fiddlers descending into their burrows, and in my dodging rush-hour traffic, crossing the beach road.

*C*olorful trumpet vines are blooming later than usual this year, their sweet scents attracting quantities of honey bees. "Who doesn't love . . . the flaming trumpet vine," wrote the poet Mary Oliver, "where the hummingbird comes, like a small green angel . . . ?"* The creeper vine, it seems, prefers tree trunks to display its five-lobed, funnel-shaped, brilliantly colored blossoms in reds and oranges. May they continue to bloom until winter!

*"Hummingbird Pauses at the Trumpet Vine;" *New and Selected Poems by Mary Oliver*; Beacon Press, Boston (1992).

*F*or gulls and for fiddler crabs
it is a game of "hide and seek."
Gulls are especially watchful this morning for
fiddler crabs, emerging from their holes in the
sand beach. A succulent meal for shorebirds,
fiddlers are delicacies. It is a deadly game—
one of life or death for the little crabs, as they
scamper back into their burrows. They have
become quite adept at escaping. Once inside
its hole, a fiddler is impregnable,
completely safe.

*T*here is a patch of pretty wildflowers growing at the foot of the seawall, hidden from view. Growing in an area that cannot be seen from the beach road, the flowers will live, bloom, and expire away from human eyes. Is their beauty diminished because they are not seen? "The little, yellow flowers that nobody notices on the edge of the road," remarked Thomas Merton, "are saints, looking up into the face of God."*

A Book of Hours by Thomas Merton; Sorin Books; Notre Dame, Indiana (2007).

*I*n a barren lot by the beach road, a young oak tree has sprouted. Around it once stood mature, damaged, dying, or dead trees, punished by the hurricane. The lot itself was the site of a handsome, ruined home, its last vestiges removed by cleanup crews. Only inches high, the sprig seeks full sunshine with uplifted leaves. A sign of renewal, the young tree has sprung from an acorn, its growth unassisted by human hands, replacing its departed elders.

The cloud bank far to the south above the barrier island is dark and menacing, indicating the approach of a common summer squall. Yet if one gives his imagination full rein, the clouds become a mountain range in an area where no mountains exist. It is a flight of the mind, for now one sees towering peaks. As the clouds drift toward the mainland, consider Sidney Lanier's verse, " . . . What the cloud doeth; the Lord knoweth. . . ."*

*"The Cloud" by Sidney Lanier; *American Poetry*, The Library of America, New York (1993).

*E*ach of the offshore posts,
as far as one can see, is
occupied by a brown pelican.
They perch motionless
for long periods of time.
So frozen is their posture,
it is as if they were marble
sculptures. Yet we know that the pelicans are
alert and very conscious of what is happening
in the water below their perches. Single-
mindedly, they are looking for fish. And when
a suitable one appears, they will instantly
plummet into the water to seize it.

*N*ear the shoreline at daybreak a large blue crab moves along slowly. Its imprints, tracks clearly visible, remain for a moment or two on the submerged sand. Then the impressions disappear, erased by waves and currents.

It is as if the crab had never been there; all evidence of its presence suddenly vanishes. It is reminiscent of the psalm,

" . . . The wind sweeps over us and we are gone; our place knows us no more. . . ."*

*Psalm 103.

*I*t happened at mid-morning. Two gulls
captured a fiddler crab. Its end was quick and
brutal, a scene I wish I had not witnessed. We
must remember that the beach is a wild place,
governed only by natural law. Hobbes said
that the state of nature is "solitary, poor, nasty,
brutish, and short."* And so it is. The gulls
rejoin their flock; the day goes on quietly, as
if nothing violent had happened. For a while,
I stand by the fiddler's empty burrow.

*Thomas Hobbes (1588–1679).

*T*wo fish crows
converse this afternoon.
"Ka, ka, ka," one says; the other
responds, "Ka, ka." Anne Porter once wrote
that they speak "with one another in a strange
tribal language . . . ."* A bit smaller than
American crows, they are smarter, too, I think.
Seldom are they trapped. Unlike other shorebirds—skimmers and gulls, to name two—fish
crows never respond to humans who imitate
their hoarse, nasal cries. We don't speak their
language.

*"Listening to the Crows" by Anne Porter; *Time's River*; Little, Brown
and Company, Boston (1999).

*A*longside the seawall are weed patches, gatherings of scores of different plants, some of which produce little flowers, yellow and red blossoms. Through the years, weeds have been defined as unwanted plants. But F.C. King has contended that "Weeds have always been condemned with-out a fair trial."* This morning allow me to speak in defense of  weeds. I call as my first witness a bedraggled plant upon which grows a golden aster.

Field Guide to Weeds by Lawrence J. Crockett; Sterling Publishing Co., New York (2003).

These are happy days for gulls! They perch serenely on offshore posts, places usually occupied by larger birds. Pelicans are now absent from our beach, because it is nesting season on the barrier islands. Not only is the female needed during the four-week incubation period, it is the role of the male to turn the eggs gently in the nest, ensuring their healthy growth. When the chicks have hatched and are flying on their own, our pelicans will return.

A tree trunk has come ashore, one end still floating, the other beached. It is not unusual for driftwood to be riddled with teredos' tunnels, but this particular tree has been consumed by the crustaceans, "termites of the sea." Imagine, if you will, the terror among Columbus' sailors, thousands of miles away from home, when they had to abandon the

Pinta,* demolished by "ship worms," the same dreaded teredos that attacked our tree trunk.

*The smallest of Columbus' three ships.

*N*esting high in a hurricane-wounded oak tree beside the beach road is a family of ospreys. If there is royalty in the kingdom of shorebirds, surely ospreys are among the most noble. Their august presence, overlooking the sea, is a happy sight. The species name in Latin is "sea eagle," and indeed they resemble eagles. We see an osprey dive, talons first, into the water with a great splash, then watch it fly back to the nest with a large mullet.

*O*ur civilization is no longer in touch with nature, especially if it is out of touch with night. " . . . With lights and ever more lights, we drive the holiness and beauty of night back into the forests and the sea . . . ," wrote Henry Beston.* Unlike in daylight hours, tonight our silent, dark beach is empty of people. They are missing the shoreline at its most peaceful moments, now illuminated only by the glow of a host of stars and a pale, sickle moon.

*The Outermost House by Henry Beston; Henry Holt & Co., Inc., New York (1929).

During a pleasant walk today at water's edge, we take note of how lucky we are. This is a place where fish swim, birds fly, insects swarm, wildflowers flourish and little fiddler crabs scurry—all with only slight interference from humans. Although an urban beach, this shoreline is still nature's wild frontier. With an impending building boom in the hurricane's aftermath, the beach must be protected from an onslaught of cement and asphalt.

*T*wo young boys play on the beach this after-noon, building sand castles, throwing shells into the waves, chasing roosting gulls, doing things that little boys do. As Walt Whitman  once observed, these days become an integral part of a child. "The horizon's edge, the flying sea-crow, the fragrance of salt marsh and shore mud . . ." all are part of a child's education.* And these things become a part of him to be remembered and savored through life.

*"There was a child went forth," *The Complete Poems of Walt Whitman;* Wordsworth Poetry Library; Ware, England (1995).

Also by George Thatcher:

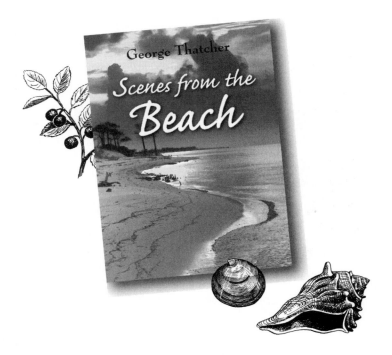

Scenes from the Beach

ISBN-13: 978-1-893062-52-8 • ISBN-10: 1-893062-52-X
5¼ x 7¼ inches • 224 pages • Hardbound • $9.95

Q QUAIL RIDGE PRESS

P. O. Box 123 • Brandon, Mississippi 39043
601-825-2063 • 800-343-1583 • www.quailridge.com